Discover and Share

Dinosaurs

Deborah Chancellor

W

FRANKLIN WATTS
LONDON • SYDNEY

About this book

The **Discover and Share** series enables young readers to read about familiar topics independently. The books are designed to build on children's existing knowledge while providing new information and vocabulary. By sharing this book, either with an adult or another child, young children can learn how to access information, build word recognition skills and develop reading confidence in an enjoyable way.

Reading tips

- Begin by finding out what children already know about the topic. Encourage them to talk about it and take the opportunity to introduce vocabulary specific to the topic.

- Each image is explained through two levels of text. Confident readers will be able to read the higher level text independently, while emerging readers can try reading the simpler sentences.

- Check for understanding of any unfamiliar words and concepts. Inexperienced readers might need you to read some or all of the text to them. Encourage children to retell the information in their own words.

- After you have explored the book together, try the quiz on page 22 to see what children can remember and to encourage further discussion.

Contents

Words in **bold** are in the glossary on page 23.

Finding dinosaurs

Huge creatures called dinosaurs roamed the Earth over 65 million years ago.

We know about dinosaurs from their fossils. Fossils are the hard **remains** of animals that lived a very long time ago. Fossils are found in rock.

People dig up fossils to find out
more about dinosaurs.

Dinosaurs
lived a very
long time ago.
We find dinosaur
fossils in
rock.

Baby dinosaurs

Dinosaurs were **reptiles**. They laid eggs, just like reptiles do today.

A dinosaur called Maiasaura laid about 30 eggs in her nest.

She looked after her **hatchlings** until they grew big enough to leave the nest.

Dinosaurs laid eggs in nests. Some of them looked after their babies very well.

Gentle giant

Some dinosaurs were enormous. Diplodocus was about 27 metres from head to tail.

That is as long as five elephants standing in a line!

Diplodocus was a **vegetarian.** It used its long neck to reach treetops, or to graze on low plants.

Some dinosaurs were very big. Some were even longer than five elephants standing in a line!

Bone cruncher

This scary dinosaur had very big jaws.

Its teeth were long and sharp.

10

Tyrannosaurus rex was a very fierce dinosaur. It had up to 60 long, sharp teeth in its strong jaws.

This powerful **carnivore** could bite through bone. We know this because the crushed bones of its **prey** have been found in its **dung.**

Fighting machine

Some dinosaurs were good at **defending** themselves from **predators**.

Ankylosaurus had tough **armour** all over its back and sides.

If Ankylosaurus was attacked,
it swung its tail club
at the enemy.

**Some dinosaurs had thick body armour.
They were hard to attack.**

Quick getaway

Some dinosaurs ran fast on their two back legs. They ran away from other dinosaurs.

14

For some dinosaurs, running was
the only way to escape from danger.
Gallimimus ran as fast as a cheetah,
at up to 95 kilometres per hour.

Gallimimus' long back legs were built for speed.
Its tail helped it to balance during quick turns.   15

Living together

Some dinosaurs lived in groups called herds. There were many dangerous predators around, so it was safer to stick together.

Parasaurolophus used its head **crest** to keep in touch with the herd. The loud honking call it made could be heard from a long way away!

Some dinosaurs lived
in groups called herds.
This helped to keep them safe.

Sea monster

Dinosaurs lived on dry land, and not in the sea.

The oceans were full of many other giant reptiles, like Elasmosaurus.

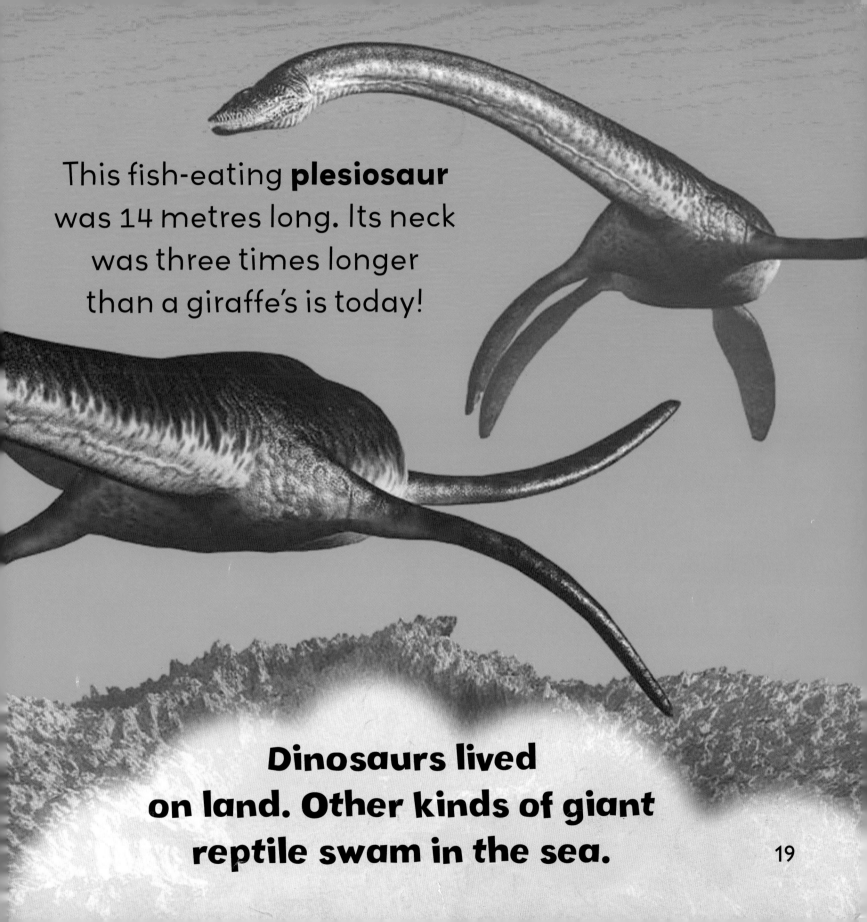

This fish-eating **plesiosaur** was 14 metres long. Its neck was three times longer than a giraffe's is today!

Dinosaurs lived on land. Other kinds of giant reptile swam in the sea.

Early bird

Many **scientists** think a small dinosaur called Archaeopteryx was the first bird.

It had teeth, claws and a bony tail like other dinosaurs, but it also had feathers and wings like a bird. It could probably fly, but not very far or well.

This dinosaur had feathers and wings. It may have been the first bird.

Quiz

1. Where do we find fossils?

2. How many teeth could a Tyrannosaurus Rex have?

3. Why did some dinosaurs have armour?

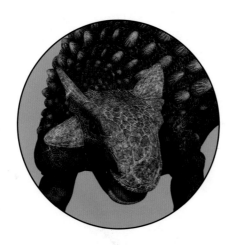

4. Why did some dinosaurs live in herds?

Glossary

armour a tough outer layer that protects an animal
carnivore an animal that only eats meat
crest a ridge of skin or feathers
defend to keep safe
dung animal poo
hatchling an animal that has hatched from an egg
plesiosaur a long-necked sea reptile
predator an animal that hunts other animals
prey an animal that is hunted by other animals
remains the parts of something that are left behind when the rest has disappeared
reptile a scaly animal that lays eggs
scientist someone who finds out about the world
vegetarian an animal that only eats plants

Answers to the quiz:
1. In rock.
2. Up to 60.
3. To protect themselves from attack.
4. To keep safe from predators.

23

Index

First published in 2015 by
Franklin Watts
338 Euston Road
London
NW1 3BH

Franklin Watts Australia
Level 17/207 Kent Street
Sydney
NSW 2000

Copyright © Franklin Watts 2015

HB ISBN 978 1 4451 3801 5
Library ebook ISBN 978 1 4451 3802 2

Dewey number: 567.9

A CIP catalogue record for this book is
available from the British Library.

Series Editor: Julia Bird
Series Advisor: Karina Law
Series Design: Basement68

Picture credits: Gualtiero Boffi/Shutterstock: 8 inset. Linda Bucklin/Shutterstock: 8,
20, 23. Leonello Calvetti/Shutterstock: 14. David Herraez Calzada/Shutterstock: 11,
22tr. Catmando/Shutterstock: 1, 7, 9, 13, 17, 22bl, 22br. Roderick Chen/Alamy: 5, 22tl.
Valentyna Chukhlyebova/Dreamstime: front cover. CreativeNature.nl/Shutterstock:
front cover b/g. dimair/Shutterstock: 4. DM7/Shutterstock: 2, 10. Corey Ford/
Stocktrek/Alamy: 19. Jean-Michel Girard/Shutterstock: 16. Mas Pix/Alamy:
3b,12. Andreas Meyer/Shutterstock: 3c, 18, 21. Prisma Archivo/Alamy:
3t, 6. Pton/Dreamstime: 15.

Every attempt has been made to clear copyright. Should there be any
inadvertent omission please apply to the publisher for rectification.

Printed in China

Franklin Watts is a division of
Hachette Children's Books,
an Hachette UK company.
www.hachette.co.uk